OTHER BOOKS BY MARY E. CARTER

A Non-Swimmer Considers Her Mikvah

I, Sarah Steinway

All Good Tova Goodman Revised Edition

The Three-Day Departure of Mrs. Annette Zinn

Diaspora of the Discombobulated

A Death Delayed — Agent Orange: Hidden Killer in Vietnam

Electronic Highway Robbery

TOVAH
MIRIAM

TOVAH
MIRIAM

A Non-Swimmer Plunges Deeper Into Her Mikvah

———

Surviving the Unfathomable Depths of October 7, 2023

——— ESSAY ———

Mary E. Carter

TOVAH
MIRIAM

A Non-Swimmer Plunges Deeper Into Her Mikvah

Surviving the Unfathomable Depths of October 7, 2023

By Mary E. Carter

This is a work of non-fiction.

Mary E. Carter

ISBN 979-8-218-47316-7

First Printing — Printed in USA

TOVAH
MIRIAM

Publisher: Tovah Miriam

www.mary-carter.com

Cover photograph: Shutterstock
Author photograph: Mary E. Carter
Book Design: Gary W. Priester

Author's Foreword

I KNOW THAT THERE IS a track in the background of my life's melodies right now. A miscued drumbeat, erratic and loud, forcing me to shake to its diabolical rhythm. A fierce drumbeat. A drumbeat of hatred. Let's not be shy. This drumbeat has lyrics to match. Words that shadow me every day since October 7, 2023. And the phrase "since October 7th" is a stubborn mantra in the back, and in the front, of my mind now – every day. My safe world, thus far, is no more. This essay is either about my admirable heroism or about my absolute recklessness.

But still, as Hillel said:

"If not now, when?"

CONTENTS

A Man With a Gun

TWELVE YEARS AGO I found my Jewish voice in five feet of water. Splashing up from my mikvah, I laughed. Non-swimmer that I had been, I was soaked and joyous. Yet I did not drown. Jewish that I had become, I was flooded with words. What followed has been a dozen years of my writing Jewish words for Jewish readers.

It was a requirement for my commitment to Judaism that I take a dip in the mikvah, an ancient symbolic ceremony which I would have to perform, in front of witnesses, protected by nothing but my own skin, in affirmation of my decision to become a Jew. Along with the classes, the books, the study, the commitments, the solemn vows, and creating my own Hebrew name, I had to immerse myself into a mikvah pool, not once, but three times, to dip my entire head under the water, hair and all, and to lift up my feet from the bottom of the pool and to float under the water in a physical act of the sanctification of my new life as Tovah Miriam. But I could not swim. Worse: I was afraid of water. Here I was about to become a stranger in a strange land and now they wanted me to dip into a strange substance as well!

What I discovered was not that I was afraid of water, but that my nervous system was. In theory, I was afraid of nothing. And, specifically, I was not at all afraid of my decision to become Jewish. But my imagination of the water engulfing me, filling my eardrums, deafening and surrounding me, alone as I would have to be in the mikvah pool; I was engulfed in an incomprehensible claustrophobia. I feared that I might panic in a spasm of my autonomic nervous system's fear of drowning. My fear was at once removed from my rational self and from my soul. And, worse, my fear was childish and embarrassing. Here I was more than fifty years of age and I was still afraid of water. Silly, really. But it was my very real fear.

Back then, in the weeks before my mikvah, I realized that there may be something valuable in my fear of water. Perhaps my fear of water had given me a unique insight into what it is to be Jewish. Without my own fears of being immersed under water, I could not have understood the all-encompassing bodily response of fear. Has not fear been with the Jews for thousands of years? The jackboots in the night. The fires of hatred. The pogroms. The camps. Make no mistake: I do not mean to diminish or trivialize the historic fears of the Jews with comparison to my own small irrational fear of being out of my depth in the mikvah.

Yet, surely, if the Jews could live through that, and other horrors unimaginable, I can do this. If Jews have survived these horrors, profound, unutterable, unceasingly in their repetition over generations, and now ingrained into the Jewish psyche, then surely — surely! — I can take my little fears and bear them into the waters of my mikvah.

The day of my mikvah I was buoyant, both in body and in my whole being.

"Did I do it? Did I do it?"

The women attending my mikvah were smiling, "Yes, you did it! Yes!"

And so the gradual full-embodiment of my Jewish self began. Eventually, I would discover that my immersion into Judaism would become much more than skin deep.

There is more to becoming Jewish than commitment to Torah. This is how my Jewish brain, gut, tongue, and very bones have evolved through

these past dozen years. Rather than just becoming a
con, as one who turns against something, I became,
rather, a pro, someone who grew into being fully
embodied, literally, and I said yes to all Jewish culture,
history, and memory. I was there at Mount Sinai, after
all, when the covenant was handed down:

> *"I make this covenant, with its sanctions, not
> with you alone, but both with those who are
> standing here with us this day before our God
> and with those who are not with us here this
> day." Deuteronomy 29:13*

Not surprisingly the process of full embodiment of
my Jewish self takes its own time to grow. It takes
place during these past twelve years. Two events stand
out. The first had its genesis in a gift from my mother
and the latest has had its birth in recent world events.

What follows here, is my narrative of these two
formative events:

One: how I approached and got rid of a man with
a gun in our synagogue parking lot.

Two: how the vicious pogrom of October 7th, 2023
shoved antisemitism directly into my own psyche. The
ramifications, foul and negative and hurtful, personal,
cruel, words spat to mock my anxious pain. That
bloody pogrom launched what I ruefully call: my

Ph.D. in my Jewish self.

Residing for these dozen years in the comfy diaspora of Reform Judaism in America, I missed entirely the toughening of my soul to endure, right into my face, words of antisemitism. Friends, so-called, now former, telling me a thing or two about my Jewish self. Saying that I lie. Saying they will generously pray for me, for my people, against our, my, very selves. We will pray. Mockery. Sarcasm. Well, I suppose I should be grateful for words, mere words. Words can't kill you.

No.

That is not true.

Words, in haste, with unexpected candor, words now tell me the truth about my smart, witty, clever, friends. With friends like these who needs enemies. Isn't that the truth? So trite. So true, I am sad to report. Antisemitism — the handy hatred, tripping off the tongue from the unimagined depths of those who said, they vowed, they did, that they had long ago left off with their Sunday-schooled selves. Lapsed catholic. Reformed Baptist. Now I discover what 'reformed' means.

Having experienced these two formative events, I am now, more than ever perhaps, flooded with words.

After my mikvah I seized a dozen years to write Jewish words for Jewish readers, mainly Jewish-themed fiction. All of my books have received awards and positive reviews.

Now it is time for me to tell the story of how I used more words to get rid of a man with a gun in our synagogue parking lot. It begins with my words, shouting.

~~~

My mother was a Gunnery Instructor in the U. S. Navy during World War II. As a teenager I asked her about the so-called indoctrination about heaven and hell. She responded with: "Oh, honey. It doesn't work that way." Her simple words of declaration opened the doors of my mind. I never went to church again. Little did I know that my pistol-packin' mother's gift of fearless words would one day help me get rid of a man with a gun in front of my own synagogue.

~~~

It starts simple:

Once upon a time there was man with a gun over there.

On a Friday, January 20th in 2017, I steered my car

into our synagogue parking lot. I was a few minutes early for a Torah Study class that I had been attending for several seasons.

Another car pulled into the space next to my driver's side. That would have been nothing unusual as our class included about a half dozen regulars. Also, we shared our Friday venue at the synagogue with another, secular, group. Other cars would soon be coming into the parking lot for both gatherings.

Glancing to my left, I watched as the driver of the car next to me got out of his car. He opened the rear door of his car, on the driver's side of his vehicle, and started to buckle up a large belt around his waist. Then he reached into the back seat and picked up a handgun. I saw the weapon as he slid it into his holster. It was a man with a gun over there.

Without hesitation, I got out of my car and strode right up to him using a certain tone, an ornery shout, and I yelled right into his face:

"WHAT ARE YOU DOING?"

Then I kept yelling:

"You can't do that here! This is a synagogue!"

He started chattering — scattered, nervous — telling me something not very coherent about being in our parking lot to rendezvous with some other officers for something that I couldn't quite make out. I asked for his identification. He handed me a very beat up wallet with a beat up looking piece of printed matter and a battered badge that I did not recognize as any kind of badge I had ever seen before. I handed the wallet back to him and said,

"This doesn't mean anything to me!"

Then he asked if I minded if he loaded another weapon. Unbelievable! And I shouted again:

"YOU CAN'T DO THAT HERE. THIS IS A SYNAGOGUE."

He asked if I minded if he parked along the street, at the curb directly in front of our parking lot. I cannot remember exactly what I said — something to the effect of 'suit yourself.' As he pulled his car around, I walked behind it and jotted down the car's license plate number.

Then he parked his car over onto the side street right next to our synagogue parking lot.

At that point my other study partners started arriving. I told them about the man. He was now in his car, parked directly adjacent to our parking lot, on the street, about twenty feet away from us. We decided to immediately leave the premises. We knew that the building was locked because the administrator had locked up and was doing errands off-site. One of our group informed the other study group members about the situation and they left too. Our group drove up the street to a restaurant where I called 911 and reported the 'a man with a gun over there.'

No police ever showed up to our synagogue to check things out.

Now here's the thing:

I simply got out of my car and approached a man with a gun. I did not rationalize. I was not afraid. I acted.

The absence of fear in my autonomic nervous system at that moment demonstrated to me exactly how much beyond rationality, how beyond fear, my action must be. And how beyond skin deep, my mikvah had taken me. And thus, the embodiment of something quite unsuspected had embraced my Jewish self: fearlessness. I was not afraid.

Of course, I had already embraced my Jewish life — in study, in observances, the annual recital of the *Al Chet*, a new me under the Huppah, my new name at the mikvah. And in what I sometimes call bashert, the Torah portion on the day of my birth was Lech L'echa:

"Go from your land, from your birthplace and from your father's house, to the land which I will show you."

And now, with a man right over there, a man with a gun, my Jewish life was about to confront me with its needs. Now the test. I aimed my Jewish self, point blank, at a man with a gun and I yelled: "WHAT ARE YOU DOING?"

I discovered that my Jewish embodiment combined conscious thought with reflexes, with instinct, brain with muscle. My Jewish mind was about to become reflexive rather than merely reflective. I got out of my car. I walked right up to a man with a gun. I hollered at him.

It was later, much later, that I thought about what I had done.

I saw a man with a gun. He intruded into my Jewish life. He did not belong here. He was danger. I got up. Walked over. I mouthed off at him. Got his license plate number. He moved his car.

Not for a moment had I been afraid. Not at that moment. And not ever since. And not now. Not today as I tell my story here.

My body just acted. I got out of my car. I approached the man. I was not afraid. I was doing what my senses and my brain and my mind and even of my years of Torah study had embodied in me to do. I acted. I shouted. I shifted from rationalism to reflex.

Step by step, my Jewish life had embodied itself in me that day.

Afterwards, my friends from Torah class, bless each and every one of them, they yelled at me:

"Don't ever do that again!"

I cannot honestly say I would never do that again. Any more than I cannot slam on the brakes if a dog runs in front of my car. Any more than a Mama Lion cannot lash out at a threat to her kittens. No. I can't promise I would not do that again.

There was a man. Over there. With a gun. That was that.

Later, another friend called me. She had a dear friend who was, at that moment, dying slowly of a debilitating stroke. My friend had been sitting by her friend's bedside for several days. My friend said to me:

"You know, what you did in the parking lot — there are worse ways to die."

I acknowledge that, yes, that's true. There are many long slow painful declines which result in the death of the body, the mind, the soul.

Now there is just one more element to my telling you about the man with a gun. And it is this: I decided to write an article for one of the Jewish publications. Something along the line of instincts blooming after

Torah study, after my mikvah.

Then another friend warned me that writing and publishing something about the man with the gun could serve to lure out the crazies and might put our congregation on the target of an anti-Semitic nut-case who might want to reenact what I have described here, or worse, God forbid, to actually shoot someone. My friend is afraid of repercussions if I tell anyone about my experience.

And so I delete the name of my congregation from this essay.

I delete my city.

I delete my state.

My friend warns me that she is afraid. And this creates in me a fear of my own.

I try to obliterate this fear — not of the man with the gun. But of my fear of hurting my friend.

And so I delete my name from this essay.

And so I delete my 'self' from this essay.

And so I censor my 'self.'

And so then?

Then what?

I write nothing about my experience?

Censored by somebody else's fear of repercussions?

And I say nothing?

But I was not afraid when I approached the man with the gun. Not in the moment of my reflexive action. Nor later.

And yet, too, I understand how fear works on a body.

Yet, now I was embodied — heart, mind, soul, right into the marrow of my bones. But, if I censor myself, then who will I be?

So now, when one of my friends speaks to me carefully about her fears of 'repercussions' if I write about the man with the gun, would it truly be my fault if there were to be any repercussions to my telling my story? I wrestle with my responsibilities — my own and my responsibilities to my friends, and of course, to my own, now fearless, Jewish self.

So, now, I am warned that if I write about my experience there could be repercussions. Now I needed to beware of both the effect of the man with the gun and also beware of inciting the worst fears of my friends.

Beware of what?

Of getting shot?

Beware of repercussions?

Beware of bullets?

Beware of words?

Beware of copycats?

Of bullets?

Of blood?

Of words? Mere words?

But I ask: wouldn't I, conversely, dis-embody myself by not talking about it?

Disembodied, I am less myself.

Disembodied, I'm a ghost.

Or numb.

Victimized.

Or dead.

There's no winning this one. Gun or no gun, I could be disembodied either way. Disembodied by his gun. Or disembodied by my own silence if I am too afraid to talk or write about the man with a gun over there.

But you've read this far. Where should I come out on this?

See what I mean? I am still wrestling with that man and his gun.

〰

I have never liked the word convert. And, in fact, I have bristled under it many times. I have overheard classmates from Torah classes say to one another out

in the parking lot: "Well, she's only a Con-Vert. What
does she know?" I have heard people say this of others
of my kin, so-called. As if that single noun, along with
its words of warning — what does she know? — is the
only word that can attach to me.

And so I never use it on myself. And, in so doing, I
excerpt that word from my most cherished
embodiment — that of having *decided* — by freewill,
with study, with commitment, with all intention — I
decided to become Jewish. Then, later, gradually, I
embodied it, all of it, surprising myself even, fearlessly
and with my every action, I embodied my Jewish self.
Not con anything, but pro every bit of it.

ANOTHER AND ANOTHER

YET THERE WAS STILL MORE that I was to learn from even more men with even more guns.

There is a Pogrom in my current lifetime.

October 7, 2023.

Here we go again. Right now.

Here comes a new life's lesson for me.

This one shoots me in the psyche.

A Pogrom. Now. In this lifetime.

In my lifetime.

Now I will learn to embody blame and aggression, shot point-blank, directly at me. I will learn, within just a very few days of a murderous act, I will learn antisemitism. I will learn it, personally, quickly, by surprise attack, I will learn that no matter what I do as a Jew I will be blamed, despised, threatened.

And, as a Jew I will be asked:

Why didn't you protect yourself?

Why didn't you do something?

Why, instead, didn't you fight back?

What? You fought back? Too much. You are too violent.

See?

You cannot win if you are the Jew. This I discover now, in the days and weeks past October 7th.

Me, an embodied Jewish woman, stepping out of the mikvah. I had not yet internalized hatred.

The Pogrom of October 7th, 2023, shot point blank into my brain, my heart, into my very bones, the solid structure of my earthly actions, walking up to and confronting danger on my own two feet, then shouting. This Pogrom got under my skin with its evil intention. Now what do I do? I had the courage to mouth off to a man with his gun not two feet from my own guts, yet I summoned the guts to shout at him. I yelled at him: "WHAT ARE YOU DOING?"

And I lucked out, I suppose. But I did it, I made a stand. So now what, Tovah Miriam? Now what is required of me after all these guns, bullets, blood — after all these men with guns? Now what?

"The way that I read it this year in light of Oct. 7
is that there are certain wounds to the spirit that
are so profound that they actually prompt a

> *fundamental change in our identity. That once this wound hits, we see ourselves differently than we did before, a shift in our own self understanding."*
>
> — Rabbi Sharon Brous, Ikar Los Angeles

Now I experience my first personal moments of antisemitism: the indifferent equivocation of a former loving friend. She shrugs. She ignores my pain, the pain I feel to my very marrow, the pain of that pogrom October 7, 2023. My friend, so-called, but not any more, ignores my Jewish pain. She equivocates. Will not commit empathy to me, her friend.

But she prays.

Thoughts and prayers.

She is, no longer, my friend.

And the daily news, the internet, moment to moment, every day, tells me that all over the globe there are people who will hate me, will take aim at me even more than that man did with his gun in my synagogue parking lot.

My head spins. My heart aches.

My heart says one thing. My brain says another. Uncertainty taints even my very clear actions back when I confronted the man with his gun. I am dizzy

with my own conflicting effects: that of my
instantaneous visceral action and that of conflicting
reactions imposed later upon my consciousness by
friends, my loving and beloved friends, so-called, and
by strangers, continents away from me. My head spins.
My heart aches. This much, however, is certain, I am
not loved, but hated. And listen to this:

Now synagogues in my state are having meetings
with FBI and local police forces and private guard
organizations, to protect our grounds and parking lots
during classes and services. Now we have guards
around our synagogue parking lots to protect us from
men with guns.

Ironic, isn't it? Guards with guns in my synagogue
parking lot. No need for Tovah Miriam to step up
now. Right?

I had already passed my trial by fire when I fired off
my mouth with:

"WHAT ARE YOU DOING?"

I yelled at that man with his gun. All those years ago.

But now this: leavened with a taste of bitter
antisemitism, the strong backbone of my words grows
stronger, not less so. Not less so. Stronger.

I am not going to shut up just because angry voices
spew at me. As my brave mother said when she aimed

her words at me about the existence of heaven and hell:

"It doesn't work that way."

Next time I meet a man with a gun, or hear words of discordant antisemitism, I have words. I am stronger now. And I will not shut up. It doesn't work that way.

Years ago, I shouted at that man with his gun in our synagogue parking lot:

"WHAT ARE YOU DOING?"

And I shall shout, again and again, to all the men with their guns and to hatred and to enormous anti-Semitic crowds all over the globe I will shout, as many times as it takes:

"HEY! WHAT ARE YOU DOING?"

"It is not incumbent upon us to finish the task, but neither are we free to desist from it altogether."
Mishnah Avot 2:16

ALMOST UNBEARABLE

THERE WAS ONE OTHER TIME in my life when the news was so stunning, so shocking, so without precedent during my short human tenure and simplistic teenage intellect, lacking as it was back then with knowledge of calumny. When that event took place, it was almost unbearable, virtually unbelievable for me. Just as October 7th has been for me.

There was news on that day November 22, 1963 that left me with physical pain in my chest, shortness of breath, disbelief from the interior of my guts to the exterior of my own baffled twisted physiognomy. Do I cry? Do I scream? Other girls in the dorm are crying and screaming on that day. The voice on radios, turned up full blast, blares the unimaginable. Repeats and repeats. Elaborates, sows further confusion. The kid running across the shady quad yells it too:

"The President's been shot. The President's been shot."

Me with my Zoology textbook clutched to my chest. I kept that textbook. All these years, I kept it. *Integrated Principles of Zoology* by Cleveland P. Hickman, Ph.D. 1961. Toted it from my first chilly apartment to the dashing Frank Lloyd Wright-type house of my middle years and all the way here to New Mexico, cossetted in retirement. Sort of. I have placed that textbook between Mark Twain and Simone DuBouvoir and Colette and then to Torah. I toted it from life to life. Self to self. Sales girl. Fashion editor. Advertising copywriter. Toted that heavy Zoo text from here to there alongside my evolving selfhood. Battered by news, news, and more news as those years spun past. All the way up to now, up to today. Until the news is so rat-a-tat-tat, blaring at me from the glowing screen of my 3:00 AM computer, linking me to unbearable news, more and more and more of it.

When did this all start?

This October 7, 2023?

I say it could have started with subtle jabs of what I now can name — finally I see it — it started with Domestic Antisemitism disguised as everyday palaver, mundane chit chat. Quite a leap, yes? But it has imbued my mind and my soul, much of it unnoticed as it spread from tabletop to pointblank attack. But now

I am much evolved since my mikvah when I could
fearlessly shout at a man with a gun:
   "HEY! WHAT ARE YOU DOING?"
   Suddenly and finally, I understand that Domestic
Antisemitism has done its work throughout my now
rather long yet oblivious little lifetime. It's subtle. It's
pervasive. Numbing. How small my life has been,
cosseted within the sunny beachy California fifties
trivia of boyfriends and final exams and the grown-
ups' expectations. Stupid. Stupid. Muffled impressions
of my particular and thus far very safe Diaspora —
protected, over-protected, so much so that I missed the
messages as they accrued, year after year, from back
then to right now. Reseda. Van Nuys. Woodland Hills.
   Baffled inside of my ever-evolving self was festering
what I now can see and name — retrospectively
unfortunately — I call it Domestic Antisemitism.
   Trying to understand '*domestic*' antisemitism —
not from historic perspectives and not from a scholarly
perspective and not from political perspectives and not
from statistical perspectives — I will discuss everyday
middle class United States neighborhood diaspora of
privileged Jews who have been spared day to day
antisemitism until recently and after Oct 7, 2023.
   Did I even notice those lurking forms of Domestic

Antisemitism? What, indeed, was that brand of antisemitism? How did it take shape in those innocent lives of Woodland Hills California? In 50's Beverly Hills? How 'bout those Christmas Tree Jews, observed and aptly named by Nora Ephron? Can't join your country club? We will build our own.

For perspective, Domestic Antisemitism has resided inside Jewish humor, hidden in glib jokey asides by Jews themselves, telling it on ourselves. It's a joke, you see. Familiar laughter exposes the antisemitism hidden in everyday Jewish life. Spewed from inside our comfortable Diaspora. It's funny. We laugh. Yet there it is. Here's a sample with a quote from my own book *A Non-Swimmer Considers Her Mikvah*, WINNER 2016 New Mexico-Arizona Book Awards Religious Category:

> *"Gary's uncle recounts the apocryphal family story of how he bought their big house in Beverly Hills. Back in the fifties in Beverly Hills, Gary's uncle was looking at a house that was for sale on Sunset. During the tour of the rooms, the owner of the house said to Gary's uncle that he'd sell him the house for less than he was offered by another man who was a Jew. This was the same*

*smug anti-Semitism of the era, the same words
that my grandmother had used to describe the
man who sold her regrooved tires back in 1945.
Only this time it's Gary's uncle who's telling the
story about himself and he's laughing. He's
laughing because the owner of the house did not
realize that Gary's uncle was Jewish too. Gary's
uncle bought the house. He was pleased with
himself for putting one over on the guy. A Jew
bought the house anyway."*

At many family gatherings, Gary's uncle retold the
story. And always with gales of rueful laughter during
those cosseted 50s.

Not so funny now, after October 7, 2023. This new
brand of antisemitism is armed. It is bitter. Aimed
point blank. Is meant to do harm. "T'aint funny
McGee."

As recently as 2019 I experienced Domestic
Antisemitism. Thanksgiving dinner. A table laden with
turkey and dressing and mashed potatoes and green
veggies and with glib antisemitism as one of the
company cheerfully says,

"Well everybody knows the Jews killed Christ."
Silence.

End of friendship as my husband and I choke down those words.

When I consider Domestic Antisemitism, situations like that come to mind. Small, living room episodes. Plain English. Words. Only words. Words can't kill you. It's just words.

Wrong.

Words can kill.

And they did during that homey Thanksgiving dinner.

Can kill.

And did.

Words, just words, powerful enough to kill. And kill they did, that friendship.

Later, right after October 7, 2023, other words came to kill.

It was just a mumbled remark, a sideways equivocation, questioning of me and my observation of that Pogrom. Here are the words that kill:

"Nobody knows who started this thing. How can you believe that this happened even? How do you even know who did it — nobody wore uniforms."

Domestic Antisemitism. Right in my face.

The most digitally documented Pogrom EVER? Are you kidding? And somebody says this to my face?

And suddenly I am turned to, I am the single person who must PROVE or disprove, the logistics and politics around the heinous events of this latest most obscenely documented Pogrom of all of history. Uniforms?! The friend requires of me to act as the solitary expert and witness due to my being Jewish? I am the one who must answer for those despicable psychotic videos that were circulated online in this well-recorded Pogrom of Oct. 7, 2023?

That: That is domestic antisemitism. Capital D. Capital A.

It is small. Doubt-laden. Words of skepticism. Disbelief. And I am required to fill in all the blanks. When it was words, mere, that shot straight into my post-mikvah selfhood. That. That is domestic — small, decorative, mundane sofa talk — those are words of antisemitism. Always doubt the Jew. Always question the Jew. Never, ever, provide humane sympathy to me, the Jew. Never embrace my agonizing sorrow over that Pogrom and over my first experiences of personal domestic antisemitism.

"But I was just asking an honest question. I asked Mary a question about the incident of Oct 7. I'm just interested is all. Just wondering is all."

No.

That innocent question is a barb. That questioner knows full well that this remark, "just interested" is a jab at my reliability as a Jew. It is presumed that I will lie. Obfuscate. Divert the conversation.

"Just wondering . . ."

That is not why this friend asked me about that Pogrom. By comparison, for example, nobody ever asked me for more strategic information about early Vietnam-era killings.

Another friend asked me why I was so upset — this, just a couple of days after Oct 7th. And I said:

"It was all the antisemitism I was watching unfold, just hours after the Pogrom."

This friend recommended a couple of novels I should read.

Are you kidding??

No matter what those books may be about, now they are out of date. Inappropriate. And from my friend, not a word of empathy, not an embrace, not a so-called fellow-feeling to comfort me — the Jew who suffers as the result of this latest Pogrom. Nothing except this:

"I'll pray."

And that prayer was to be for the Palestinians!!!!

Lapsed Catholic? Right. But not a peep to comfort

me for my sorrows as I watched antisemitism rise within hours of the Pogrom.

And it engulfs me. As does the sorrow and shock at losing this longtime friend.

This is what I mean by Domestic Antisemitism. Just little stuff. No matter, right? No. On the contrary.

And how do I know this? By comparison, I can put those antisemitisms in perspective from the warm and embracing calls I immediately received from two other friends whose words and tone were filled with love and deep caring about how I might be reacting to the new onslaught of hatred, aimed point-blank, at my heart as I dive deeper into my own commitment at my mikvah.

Writing about antisemitism, it is almost impossible to avoid the tone of a screed. And without the props of history, politics, scholarship, or statistics, there isn't much to say that won't reverberate ultimately with the sound of voices raised in anger, ultimate fisticuffs, threatened gunshots, brandished knives.

But, hey, words can't kill.

Can't they?

And so, as I try to explore my own small reactions to Domestic Antisemitism, there isn't much to write about. This may turn out to be a blessedly blank chapter.

Let's see.

How to proceed?

How 'bout this?:

I have tried to trace and to understand Domestic Antisemitism. The type of antisemitism that I grew up with, born as I was just before the end of WWII. Me and the atom bomb. Nursery-mates in the San Fernando Valley before freeways. What kind of genocide resulted from the dropping of those two bombs? None. So-called, that is. After all, we suffered the attack upon Pearl Harbor. How many dead back then? Yet, nowadays such a defensive move upon a sovereign nation, by another sovereign nation, would bring down a storm of accusations: genocide! UN sponsored to boot. And the twin claims voiced as mere questions, 'just asking' sort of thing:

Why didn't you protect yourself?

Oh. You did? Well then: you played too rough.

Don't go there, Mary. You will be hamstrung in tangled strands of unimaginable amendments to ancient history. Likewise: don't mention Chaco Canyon. Stay in your lane, Mary. Woodland Hills. Reseda. 1950. But what are you going to do Tovah Miriam?

Dive Deeper

It would be easy, even facile, yet certainly boring and expected — for me to write a misery memoir to show the world how hurt I have been by antisemitism lobbed at me. Oh the whining I could transform into literature! How being wronged can taint otherwise thoughtful writing. The shelves are loaded with those tomes. Everybody loves a sad sad tale. Especially penned by a woman. A woman of a certain age — Ah, even better. But I want to do it better. I want to tell my tales of harsh rejection, mean words, spiteful skepticism, spitting rage — I selfishly want to just do it better.

And then I remember — hey I have written five novels with those goals already in place. I have steered, subconsciously I suppose, into waters of midrash, of contemplation, of commentary. I woke up from a rudderless funk about what to make of October 7, 2023 and this aha experience dawned upon me:

Hey! I have already written my Jewish responses to my new Jewish life. My novels have everything I require to comfort my distress over Domestic Antisemitism — to appease my hurt heart and anger over October 7, 2023. My books, my words, can mend me. I may not be able to cure rampant, and now world-wide, antisemitism, but there is balm for its effects in my own words and stories. Respite. My own Jewish-themed books may even provide respite for my readers.

Here are samples from my own novels which contain Jewish characters and themes:

Several times a year we are asked, as an aggregation of all kinds of Jews during our High Holy Days, we are required to say, in unison, the long form recitation that is contained in our ceremony of the *Al Chet*. And whether we did or did not commit one of these forty statements, we take responsibility for the possibility that we may have harmed others with our words — mere words. And I created a fictional character in my latest novel, a Guardian Angel, who expounds, and even harps somewhat, upon how words may cause harm.

> *"I do not mean to harp. I do not speak here by way of sermonizing. But, you dear reader,*

might do well to remember, Angels are prone to harping. We are always in a flap about something.

So listen now to me.

Words, hasty and hot, can kill desire, can kill enthusiasm, can kill inspiration, aspiration, creation. Words, so-called mere words, can kill souls and deprive them of the energy needed for a soul's evolution into fulfillment. And a soul is not unlike an Angel — nobody has ever seen one. Yet a soul can be killed . . .

Just words, never mind. Can't kill you.

Right?

And one more thing:

Do not mistake words that are spoken in the name of freedom of speech as words that are somehow exempt because of some fallacious nobility of motives — do not mistake that kind of freedom with innocence or exemption from harm. Murderous phrases, threats, screamed name-calling, verbal discourtesies, regurgitations of gossip, hollering, words hissed through gritted teeth, yelled in protest, noble protest in the name of freedom of speech — all of these and nameless multitudes of other words, mere, are

capable of creating intense harm, physical and
mental. Abused by freedom, so-called, of speech.
I have a right, you know. Your righteous right,
ironic twist of good intentions — so-called — is
when words can kill most effectively. And they
will. And they have done. And they do. Kill."

Excerpts from Diaspora of the Discombobulated
©*2023 Mary E. Carter*

And then there is this. We Jews reflect upon our lives. Almost every single time we gather in our rooms, whether in minions or alone beside darkened rumpled sheets. Who shall live and who shall die? And, more to the point I sometimes wonder: when?

This question I take up in my novel *The Three-Day Departure of Mrs. Annette Zinn*. It comes with the recitation of Kaddish. We say these words as final words at the end of a Jewish life.

Here again, my forever student, a character I name Mrs. Annette Zinn, continues unto death — I kill her off on the very first page of my 2019 novel *The Three-Day Departure of Mrs. Annette Zinn* — our form of Torah study holds firm even as we step through the threshold and into the world to come and our engagement engages our attention. It can be like this from that book:

> *Blessed are You. Blessed all blessings and hymns, praises, and consolations that may be uttered in this world, in the days of our lifetime, and say, Amen.*

> *Kaddish invokes only life and never mentions death.*

> *"Now that she is about to enter the world to come, will she be able to comprehend even the hidden or forgotten details from her time in this world?*

> *Look at her: Mrs. Annette Zinn.*
> *See that she is an ordinary woman.*
> *She has had three days to review — to view again — her life.*
> *Her ninety-five years. . .*
> *Throughout it all, she was doing the best she could.*
> *Only human.*
> *Absolutely human.*
> *Facing her destination.*
> *May her memory be.*
> *Just be."*

And then, shocking, suddenly, there is a Pogrom.

October 7, 2023.

And times being insistent, time being inexorable, I am asked to create my usual beautiful fun Seder, my own beloved Haggadah. And I am blank. Stultified. Stumped. Sickened. Without words.

I did manage this bit:

Pesach starts with action, with prayer. We pray and then repeat the story of our escape from slavery. That is Pesach. Prayer does not particularly require belief. I once doubted prayer. A rabbi noticed my reluctance to pray over a loaf of challah that I had just made. He suggested to me that:

"Prayer is not about belief. It is about action. Prayer is in your mindful creation of that loaf, warm and golden, that you hold now to your heart. That is prayer for you, Tovah Miriam."

As a percentage of the Jewish population of the United States, I, as a volunteer, so-to-speak, represent only a tiny portion of the total. I am a tiny portion of the tiny totality of the Jewish population in the United States. In the world. I, who chose to study with my mikvah as my goal, became a con-vert — a word I do not like — as I entered my mikvah as a **pro** rather than as a **con** — more committed to something rather than turning **against** something else.

The first thing that happened to me after October 7, 2023 was a vicious verbal assault from two close and so-called friends. Not two days had gone by. The form and wording of their anti-Semitic blasts does not merit repetition. Feh! But it hurt. It stung. And, yes, as one of the characters of my fiction harped upon:

"Words can kill."

And they did.

And so I have entered the advanced studies program of my Jewish life. I ruefully call it my Ph.D. in my Jewish self.

Piled on top of my first experiences of personal antisemitism has been the holiday of Pesach — my favorite Jewish observance. I love making midrashic Haggadot and presenting them to friends around sometimes raucous tables loaded with enough lovingkindness for me to gorge upon. I was asked to write another of my now-modestly 'famous' Haggadot. I kvelled.

Yet this year was different.

This year was filled instead with anxiety for me. How could I create something uplifting, fun, optimistic, jammed side by side into this period of vicious onslaughts? All these things piled higher and deeper, all these months later? Delusional campus riots? Declared warfare? Lies? And lies? And lies? And more antisemitism than I had ever personally experienced before. Filled with words that kill? How could I joyfully proceed in this year 5784?

Here is what I created:

Our Final Pasach Prayer 5784

In summary: As I worked with these texts from Exodus, I realized that there are words and phrases that may be transposed into a prayer — a final prayer for this Pesach 5784. Transposed means: to rearrange, to change the relative position, order, or sequence of something — just as our world — our hearts, our guts, our lungs — have been changed and rearranged and deeply re-ordered since October 7, 2023. To review — here is our narrative, our history, from G_d in Exodus:

"I heard the moaning of the Israelites because the Egyptians are holding them in bondage . . . I will free you from that labor . . .
And deliver you from bondage.

I will redeem you with an outstretched arm . . .
I will take you for my people and . . .
You shall know I am your G_d who freed you . . ."

Today, we may — we must — rearrange these
words to make a prayer for the hostages who have
been held since October 7, 2023 in yet another land.
Let us read it now — aloud together as we recite our
final prayer of Pesach. Please read aloud with me and
raise our voices in prayer:

Again, today, other Jews are being
held as hostages . . .
free them now . . .
deliver them from bondage.
redeem them with an outstretched arm . . .
With this our prayer to G_d who freed us all,
Return them we beseech you,
On this, our Pesach 5784
Amen

Then I discovered that I had already written about
this perspective on prayer. In my Debut Novel *I, Sarah
Steinway* my character reflects upon this bit of Jewish
wisdom:

"I may have tried, but other than the prayer

of my survival, the ordinary acts — clean the
buckets, scoop the fishes — the rabbis got that
right. My survival, then, has been my prayer."

Then of course there is the conundrum of what is
the meaning of the word 'good'? It is especially potent
when juxtaposed with the word 'Pogrom'. And here
you have the sticking point. It's ridiculous, really.
Impossible. Troublesome. I wake up, twelve years past
my dip into the mikvah, and here I am, responsible for
answering for the words 'good' and 'Pogrom'. All in
one deed, I, an average Jewish person, am required to
answer for all these things. How can the Jewish
responses to Pogrom be any 'good'? Any 'good' at all?
Boy am I in for it. You. You Tovah Miriam — what say
you?

"Not only was Tova Goodman called Tova
Goodman, but her very name became her
calling. Nothing about the word good would
escape her scrutiny. From her student days, as
Tova studied Torah in the Rabbi's study, she was
compelled to question good . . . when God began
to create heaven and earth and first-off created
light and then darkness and then said it was

*"good" — well shouldn't he-she-or-it first off
define the word good?"*
From *All Good Tova Goodman Revised Edition* ©2022

Then on October 7, 2023 there is a Pogrom.
Vicious. Violent. A killing field. Hostages taken.

Within minutes into this new horror, I am required
to explain those crimes. And those horrendous crimes
were quickly transformed into 'good' responses for
heinous acts. Suddenly that Pogrom was praised as
being 'good' because those acts were perpetrated by a
band of people who had claimed, righteously,
treacherously, that they had finally 'just had enough'
and their viciousness was therefore a fair and just
response to the actions of generations of Jews. And
suddenly, I am asked to respond to this Pogrom.

"Just wondering."

You see. I am on the spot. And I tell you, my
mental struggle has caused me indescribable pain. I
am poked at, questioned in anger, accused by a whole
world of people who now take up antisemitism as their
weapon. I seek a "happy" ending. Really?

Then I wake up, a few days after Pesach 2024 and
there it is. I have already addressed these convolutions
Jewishly. In my books. My novels. "Happy" endings.

My novels have everything I need to soothe and to comfort distress I suffer over Domestic Antisemitism which has infected the whole world now with that convenient hatred — universal antisemitism.

So finally I see that my own work — my own books, with a raft of ordinary characters, Jews, who struggle with Torah, whether they realize it or not, they struggle with ordinary Jewish lives. These novels, my own works, can appease my hurt heart, quell my anger — over the Pogrom of October 7, 2023. My own work, these books, mend me, provide respite to bind my wounds after unspeakable assault. Really?

I pick up one of my books. Then another. And another. Thumbing through, I read my own words. And believe it or not, I have not read any of them in several years. And look: they are rather good! Ya done good, Tovah Miriam!

And, so it seems: I have already written from the perspective of my ordinary Jewish heart. To address this Pogrom, with its many, many, too many, obscenities, its foul horrors, and so as I struggle with how on earth I can ever address October 7, 2023 I see my work has done this already. That's good. Right?

Is it enough?

Since October 7, 2023, I have not run away from my chosen Jewish life, not hoisted myself out of the waters of my mikvah, but have instead dived ever deeper into its depths. I have made a body of work, my books, into my refuge from antisemitism. My words now serve to reinforce my pledges that bind me, ever stronger, to my chosen Jewish life. Pogrom or peacetime, here I am. Guns nor antisemitism, neither drive me under. I am here. Still. And I will shout:

"HEY! WHAT ARE YOU DOING?"

And this — *that* — is all I have to say.

— End —

AUTHOR'S AFTERWORD

IT WAS NOT A REQUIREMENT for me to be re-married Jewishly after I stepped out of my mikvah. Yet, Gary and I chose to add this observance to my commitments after the mikvah. Several years later, we set a date, invited a lively contingent of friends, hired catering for an abundant table, and designed our invitations.

Now, of course, we feast on all our friends' signatures upon our Ketubah and wonder how we gathered the courage to face that loving disparate roomful of souls. And, of course now, we wonder how to commemorate the lavish lovingkindness we harvested on that day.

In light of all of today's darkness, how could we dare to indulge in that distant day of happiness and light?

Then I remembered — I needed to look up the source — a quote from Talmud:

"If a funeral procession
and wedding procession meet at a crossroads,
which one has the right of way?
The Talmud says the wedding should lead.
We must lead with Life."

— Talmud Ketubot 17a

I realized, only recently, that I did not thank two of our guests who traveled more than a thousand miles to attend our joyous event. I think I was hungrily reminiscing about our Jewish wedding, overwhelmed as I have been lately by the pall cast over past happy moments, amidst the forces of these dark and brutal times. I came up short realizing I had not properly thanked these two guests for coming to our Jewish wedding back in 2015.

These two were friends who date back to Gary's college years and date back to the first months after Gary and I met. More than fifty years ago. These were, and are, friends who had lived very busy and committed lives as we were also experiencing our very too-busy lives with our careers and, later, with a consuming business of our own for a dozen years. Our friendships were enforced by periods of silence for months and years at a stretch. But I realized now that they had been here with us all along and that we, too, had been there, all along, with them. Engaging in Life.

It is actually Jewish Law as found in the Talmud Ketubot 17a:

*"**The Sages taught:***
*One **reroutes** the funeral procession*
*for burial of a **corpse** to yield **before** the wedding*
*procession of a **bride**."*

Thank you, dear ones, as we cherish now your presence with us during this current time in history, laden as it is with darkness. You are cherished and you well understand that we must lead with Life.

Mary E. Carter

2024 June

Mary E. Carter's Award-Winning Fiction and Non-fiction books:

- *A Non-Swimmer Considers Her Mikvah* was the 2016 WINNER Religious Book in the New Mexico-Arizona Book Awards.
- *I, Sarah Steinway*, her first novel, was a 2018 FINALIST in the National Jewish Book Awards as a Debut Novel and was also a 2018 WINNER Religious Book in the New Mexico-Arizona Book Awards.
- *The Three-Day Departure of Mrs. Annette Zinn* was a 2019 WINNER Religious Book in the New Mexico-Arizona Book Awards.
- *All Good Tova Goodman Revised Edition* was a 2022 WINNER Religious Book in the New Mexico-Arizona Book Awards.
- *Diaspora of the Discombobulated*, published July 2023, **Book of the Week**, *Albuquerque Journal*.

All books are available through Ingram & amazon or at local bookstores.

Mary E. Carter, New Mexico, USA
www.mary-carter.com

ABOUT THE AUTHOR

 Mary E. Carter's debut novel *I, Sarah Steinway* was a FINALIST in the National Jewish Book Awards, 2019, and was a WINNER in the New Mexico-Arizona Book Awards, 2018. Her novel, *The Three-Day Departure of Mrs. Annette Zinn*, and her memoir, *A Non-Swimmer Considers Her Mikvah*, were both WINNERS in the New Mexico-Arizona Book Awards.

During a twenty-five-year career, Carter was an advertising copywriter doing broadcast and print advertising at Grey Advertising, Honig-Cooper & Harrington/Foote Cone & Belding, and Erwin Wasey in Los Angeles. She and her husband had a design company in San Francisco doing corporate high technology and consumer marketing and advertising for Ernst & Young, Charles Schwab, Dreyer's, Chateau St. Jean Winery, and many others. She was born in the San Fernando Valley long before there were freeways in Southern California.

Author Mary E. Carter became Jewish after age fifty. This is her story. It is about creating a new life and making changes as an older adult. Carter discusses: finding rabbis, attending classes, studying, making a Hebrew name, and the commitment at the mikvah. This is a book for anyone thinking about becoming Jewish as an adult.

"Who knew a book about becoming Jewish could be so engaging? Carter's talent as a visual artist shows from cover to content. Vignettes, snapshots, and episodes converge in a kaleidoscopic rendering of her journey to Judaism."

—*Rabbi Deborah J. Brin*, rabbibrin.com

Available through Ingram and amazon

Sarah Steinway, aged seventy-five, survives a catastrophic flood by moving into her treehouse on the northern shoreline of the San Francisco Bay. With snark and pluck, she lives up there for five years. Turning to Torah for comfort, she instead engages in argumentation with God, shouting the eternal question: "Why me?"

"...*by turns very funny and very serious, confident and uncompromisingly weird. Mary E. Carter has a voice with unquestionable power, and we look forward to reading more from her.*"

—Jewish Book Council

Available through Ingram and amazon.

Whatever happened to Sarah Steinway? Find out in this sequel, *All Good Tova Goodman Revised Edition*. Readers will be surprised by the haunting conclusion of Mary E. Carter's Award-Winning Debut Novel, *I, Sarah Steinway*.

"Carter's page-turning portrait of a woman surviving the apocalypse is hauntingly memorable."

—— Publishers Weekly

THE
THREE-DAY DEPARTURE
of
MRS. ANNETTE ZINN

A NOVEL
MARY E. CARTER

"I always look forward to getting to know Mary E. Carter's characters. The Jews, and the righteous non-Jews as well, have a pintele yid: a spark of Jewishness that helps them navigate this complex world with sensitivity. I enjoyed the exploration of the soul hovering for three days and was intrigued with the idea that it might remember details of events that were forgotten or hidden during its time in this world. During her three-day departure, Mrs. Annette Zinn discovers that her memories have the potential to serve as a blessing."

— Rabbi Jack Shlachter
Judaism for Your Nuclear Family, physicsrabbi@gmail.com

Available through Ingram and amazon

Made in the USA
Columbia, SC
28 October 2024

44927150R00040